Daily Affirmations

Included in this journal should be repeated three times per day until you can repeat them from memory.

I have all the
strength and
confidence
within me
that I need
to succeed

This Journal Belongs to:

____

COMMUNICATION LOG

DATE:

Today we spoke and I feel:

Today we didn't speak and I feel:

Today I received a package and I feel:

Today, I didn't receive a package and I feel:

"NO ONE IS YOU, THAT IS YOUR POWER"

REFLECTIONS

DATE:

"ANYTHING WORTH HAVING TAKES TIME."

REFLECTIONS

DATE:

"ANYTHING WORTH HAVING TAKES TIME."

REFLECTIONS

DATE:

"ANYTHING WORTH HAVING TAKES TIME."

COMMUNICATION LOG

DATE:

Today we spoke and I feel:

Today we didn't speak and I feel:

Today I received a package and I feel:

Today, I didn't receive a package and I feel:

"NO ONE IS YOU, THAT IS YOUR POWER"

REFLECTIONS

DATE:

"ANYTHING WORTH HAVING TAKES TIME."

REFLECTIONS

DATE:

"ANYTHING WORTH HAVING TAKES TIME."

REFLECTIONS

DATE:

"ANYTHING WORTH HAVING TAKES TIME."

REFLECTIONS

DATE:

"ANYTHING WORTH HAVING TAKES TIME."

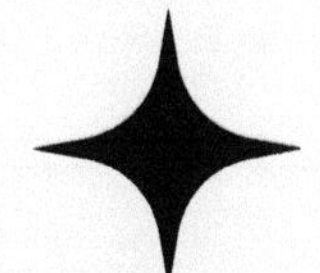

I am in
control of
my life.

COMMUNICATION LOG

DATE:

Today we spoke and I feel:

Today we didn't speak and I feel:

Today I received a package and I feel:

Today, I didn't receive a package and I feel:

"NO ONE IS YOU, THAT IS YOUR POWER"

REFLECTIONS

DATE:

"ANYTHING WORTH HAVING TAKES TIME."

REFLECTIONS

DATE:

"ANYTHING WORTH HAVING TAKES TIME."

REFLECTIONS

DATE:

"ANYTHING WORTH HAVING TAKES TIME."

COMMUNICATION LOG

DATE:

Today we spoke and I feel:

Today we didn't speak and I feel:

Today I received a package and I feel:

Today, I didn't receive a package and I feel:

"NO ONE IS YOU, THAT IS YOUR POWER"

REFLECTIONS

DATE:

"ANYTHING WORTH HAVING TAKES TIME."

REFLECTIONS

DATE:

"ANYTHING WORTH HAVING TAKES TIME."

REFLECTIONS

DATE:

"ANYTHING WORTH HAVING TAKES TIME."

REFLECTIONS

DATE:

"ANYTHING WORTH HAVING TAKES TIME."

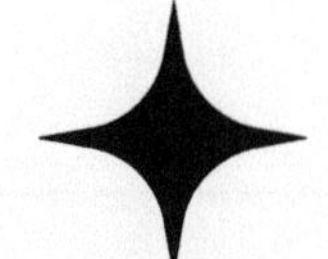

Today will be
a great day.

COMMUNICATION LOG

DATE:

Today we spoke and I feel:

Today we didn't speak and I feel:

Today I received a package and I feel:

Today, I didn't receive a package and I feel:

"NO ONE IS YOU, THAT IS YOUR POWER"

REFLECTIONS

DATE:

"ANYTHING WORTH HAVING TAKES TIME."

REFLECTIONS

DATE:

"ANYTHING WORTH HAVING TAKES TIME."

REFLECTIONS

DATE:

"ANYTHING WORTH HAVING TAKES TIME."

COMMUNICATION LOG

DATE:

Today we spoke and I feel:

Today we didn't speak and I feel:

Today I received a package and I feel:

Today, I didn't receive a package and I feel:

"NO ONE IS YOU, THAT IS YOUR POWER"

REFLECTIONS

DATE:

"ANYTHING WORTH HAVING TAKES TIME."

REFLECTIONS

DATE:

"ANYTHING WORTH HAVING TAKES TIME."

REFLECTIONS

DATE:

"ANYTHING WORTH HAVING TAKES TIME."

REFLECTIONS

DATE:

"ANYTHING WORTH HAVING TAKES TIME."

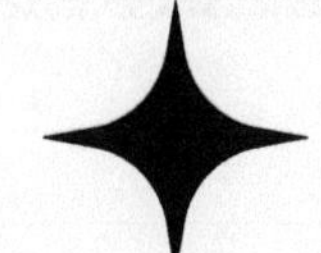

I am
awesome.

COMMUNICATION LOG

DATE:

Today we spoke and I feel:

Today we didn't speak and I feel:

Today I received a package and I feel:

Today, I didn't receive a package and I feel:

"NO ONE IS YOU, THAT IS YOUR POWER"

REFLECTIONS

DATE:

"ANYTHING WORTH HAVING TAKES TIME."

REFLECTIONS

DATE:

"ANYTHING WORTH HAVING TAKES TIME."

REFLECTIONS

DATE:

"ANYTHING WORTH HAVING TAKES TIME."

COMMUNICATION LOG

DATE:

Today we spoke and I feel:

Today we didn't speak and I feel:

Today I received a package and I feel:

Today, I didn't receive a package and I feel:

"NO ONE IS YOU, THAT IS YOUR POWER"

REFLECTIONS

DATE:

"ANYTHING WORTH HAVING TAKES TIME."

REFLECTIONS

DATE:

"ANYTHING WORTH HAVING TAKES TIME."

REFLECTIONS

DATE:

"ANYTHING WORTH HAVING TAKES TIME."

REFLECTIONS

DATE:

"ANYTHING WORTH HAVING TAKES TIME."

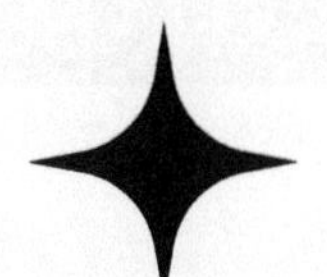

Nothing can stop me from achieving what I want

COMMUNICATION LOG

DATE:

Today we spoke and I feel:

Today we didn't speak and I feel:

Today I received a package and I feel:

Today, I didn't receive a package and I feel:

"NO ONE IS YOU, THAT IS YOUR POWER"

REFLECTIONS

DATE:

"ANYTHING WORTH HAVING TAKES TIME."

REFLECTIONS

DATE:

"ANYTHING WORTH HAVING TAKES TIME."

REFLECTIONS

DATE:

"ANYTHING WORTH HAVING TAKES TIME."

COMMUNICATION LOG

DATE:

Today we spoke and I feel:

Today we didn't speak and I feel:

Today I received a package and I feel:

Today, I didn't receive a package and I feel:

"NO ONE IS YOU, THAT IS YOUR POWER"

REFLECTIONS

DATE:

"ANYTHING WORTH HAVING TAKES TIME."

REFLECTIONS

DATE:

"ANYTHING WORTH HAVING TAKES TIME."

REFLECTIONS

DATE:

"ANYTHING WORTH HAVING TAKES TIME."

REFLECTIONS

DATE:

"ANYTHING WORTH HAVING TAKES TIME."

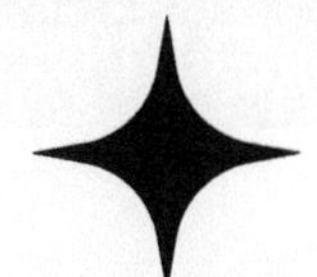

I can handle anything that comes my way.

COMMUNICATION LOG

DATE:

Today we spoke and I feel:

Today we didn't speak and I feel:

Today I received a package and I feel:

Today, I didn't receive a package and I feel:

"NO ONE IS YOU, THAT IS YOUR POWER"

REFLECTIONS

DATE:

"ANYTHING WORTH HAVING TAKES TIME."

REFLECTIONS

DATE:

"ANYTHING WORTH HAVING TAKES TIME."

REFLECTIONS

DATE:

"ANYTHING WORTH HAVING TAKES TIME."

COMMUNICATION LOG

DATE:

Today we spoke and I feel:

Today we didn't speak and I feel:

Today I received a package and I feel:

Today, I didn't receive a package and I feel:

"NO ONE IS YOU, THAT IS YOUR POWER"

REFLECTIONS

DATE:

"ANYTHING WORTH HAVING TAKES TIME."

REFLECTIONS

DATE:

"ANYTHING WORTH HAVING TAKES TIME."

REFLECTIONS

DATE:

"ANYTHING WORTH HAVING TAKES TIME."

REFLECTIONS

DATE:

"ANYTHING WORTH HAVING TAKES TIME."

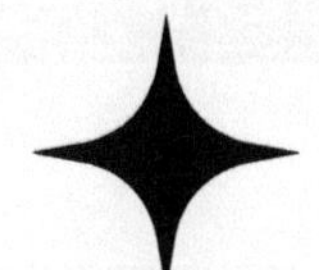

I chose faith
over fear.

COMMUNICATION LOG

DATE:

Today we spoke and I feel:

Today we didn't speak and I feel:

Today I received a package and I feel:

Today, I didn't receive a package and I feel:

"NO ONE IS YOU, THAT IS YOUR POWER"

REFLECTIONS

DATE:

"ANYTHING WORTH HAVING TAKES TIME."

REFLECTIONS

DATE:

"ANYTHING WORTH HAVING TAKES TIME."

REFLECTIONS

DATE:

"ANYTHING WORTH HAVING TAKES TIME."

COMMUNICATION LOG

DATE:

Today we spoke and I feel:

Today we didn't speak and I feel:

Today I received a package and I feel:

Today, I didn't receive a package and I feel:

"NO ONE IS YOU, THAT IS YOUR POWER"

REFLECTIONS

DATE:

"ANYTHING WORTH HAVING TAKES TIME."

REFLECTIONS

DATE:

"ANYTHING WORTH HAVING TAKES TIME."

REFLECTIONS

DATE:

"ANYTHING WORTH HAVING TAKES TIME."

REFLECTIONS

DATE:

"ANYTHING WORTH HAVING TAKES TIME."

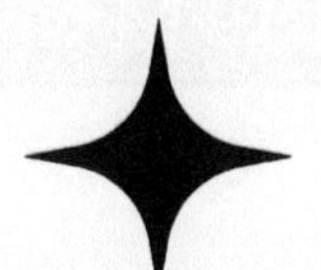

I'm willing to see things differently.

COMMUNICATION LOG

DATE:

Today we spoke and I feel:

Today we didn't speak and I feel:

Today I received a package and I feel:

Today, I didn't receive a package and I feel:

"NO ONE IS YOU, THAT IS YOUR POWER"

REFLECTIONS

DATE:

"ANYTHING WORTH HAVING TAKES TIME."

REFLECTIONS

DATE:

"ANYTHING WORTH HAVING TAKES TIME."

REFLECTIONS

DATE:

"ANYTHING WORTH HAVING TAKES TIME."

COMMUNICATION LOG

DATE:

Today we spoke and I feel:

Today we didn't speak and I feel:

Today I received a package and I feel:

Today, I didn't receive a package and I feel:

"NO ONE IS YOU, THAT IS YOUR POWER"

REFLECTIONS

DATE:

"ANYTHING WORTH HAVING TAKES TIME."

REFLECTIONS

DATE:

"ANYTHING WORTH HAVING TAKES TIME."

REFLECTIONS

DATE:

"ANYTHING WORTH HAVING TAKES TIME."

REFLECTIONS

DATE:

"ANYTHING WORTH HAVING TAKES TIME."

Everything in life happens for me.

COMMUNICATION LOG

DATE:

Today we spoke and I feel:

Today we didn't speak and I feel:

Today I received a package and I feel:

Today, I didn't receive a package and I feel:

"NO ONE IS YOU, THAT IS YOUR POWER"

REFLECTIONS

DATE:

"ANYTHING WORTH HAVING TAKES TIME."

REFLECTIONS

DATE:

"ANYTHING WORTH HAVING TAKES TIME."

REFLECTIONS

DATE:

"ANYTHING WORTH HAVING TAKES TIME."

COMMUNICATION LOG

DATE:

Today we spoke and I feel:

Today we didn't speak and I feel:

Today I received a package and I feel:

Today, I didn't receive a package and I feel:

"NO ONE IS YOU, THAT IS YOUR POWER"

REFLECTIONS

DATE:

"ANYTHING WORTH HAVING TAKES TIME."

REFLECTIONS

DATE:

"ANYTHING WORTH HAVING TAKES TIME."

REFLECTIONS

DATE:

"ANYTHING WORTH HAVING TAKES TIME."

REFLECTIONS

DATE:

"ANYTHING WORTH HAVING TAKES TIME."

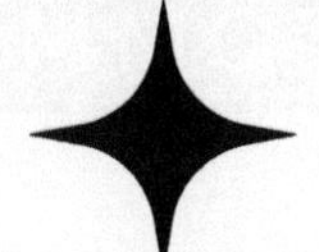

I will make today count.

COMMUNICATION LOG

DATE:

Today we spoke and I feel:

Today we didn't speak and I feel:

Today I received a package and I feel:

Today, I didn't receive a package and I feel:

"NO ONE IS YOU, THAT IS YOUR POWER"

REFLECTIONS

DATE:

"ANYTHING WORTH HAVING TAKES TIME."

REFLECTIONS

DATE:

"ANYTHING WORTH HAVING TAKES TIME."

REFLECTIONS

DATE:

"ANYTHING WORTH HAVING TAKES TIME."

REFLECTIONS

DATE:

"ANYTHING WORTH HAVING TAKES TIME."

REFLECTIONS

DATE:

"ANYTHING WORTH HAVING TAKES TIME."

REFLECTIONS

DATE:

"ANYTHING WORTH HAVING TAKES TIME."

www.ingramcontent.com/pod-product-compliance
Ingram Content Group UK Ltd.
Pitfield, Milton Keynes, MK11 3LW, UK
UKHW041929190726
13854UKWH00004B/1524

9 781794 821569